VIEWS OF OUR HISTORIC DISTRICT

GALENA, ILLINOIS

GEAR HOUSE, INC.
GALENA, ILLINOIS

ISBN 0-9653052-0-1   10-95

ACKNOWLEDGEMENTS

I would like to thank the following people who were of great help to me while researching and writing this view book. Alfred Mueller and Richard Vincent shared their old photo collections of the town with me as well as a great deal of time in answering my historical questions. Joel Dexter came to Galena on many occasions to photograph different aspects and times of the year. Dan Ahern presented creative design ideas. And, finally thanks to Daryl Watson and the Galena/Jo Daviess County Historical Society and Museum for finding those hard to place buildings and dates. Their combined creativity, help and patience was most helpful.

Susan Pettey

CONTENTS

THE HISTORIC DISTRICT OF GALENA, ILLINOIS

Galena, Illinois. Where past and present become one. From hand made brick to hand carved wood, Galena is timeless. Nestled in the far northwestern corner of Illinois, along the Mississippi River, Galena sits just as it did when its elegance and refinement came from the immense mineral and merchantile wealth produced in the region. Graceful mansions still hug the hillsides, brick buildings still line Main Street; but, a once large and forceful river is now a gentle stream. Due to its location, the town survived through the years to become an authentic glimpse into another life and time. Remarkably, Galena has one of the most intact concentrated historic districts in the country.

As a result of the lead mines scattered throughout the Wisconsin, Illinois and Iowa territories, Galena became the largest thriving river port north of St. Louis, in the 1840s and early 1850s. The mines attracted hundreds of men and their families from all over the east and south, causing Galena's economy to far surpass that of the small town to the east called Chicago. The Fever River (later renamed the Galena River in 1854) was 250 feet wide in its heyday and several large steamboats would dock at one time to unload luxury cargo, such as fine foods and drinks, furniture, fabrics and the latest products from the east and south. The boats were then reloaded with shipments of lead as well as other products for the return trip. The steamboats carried out thousands of pounds of lead a day and by 1845 Galena was producing over 80% of the nation's lead. The town took its name from the latin word meaning "lead."

Today visitors to Galena can view for themselves what this nineteenth century river and lead mine town was like. The majority of buildings in the historic district are original and have changed little since the wealthy lead mine owners, merchants, and riverboat captains first built them. The architecture of Galena is as diverse as any large city. Federal, Greek Revival, Italianate and Queen Anne are just a few of the many architectural styles lining the streets.

Galena's historic district was placed on the National Register of Historic Places on October 8, 1969, using the city limits from March 28, 1838 to December 31, 1859 as its boundaries.

This view book has been put together to give readers a look into an authentic historic town. A town which has retained its nineteenth century charm, while still maintaining a very active historic district. Old photographs, paintings, and prints are used to show what is standing today was also standing then. The four seasons bring different looks to Galena. Winter brings lights and candles glowing from mansions nestled into the snowy hillsides. The town is trimmed with nineteenth century christmas decorations; mostly greenery, red bows and white lights. The spring and summer months are filled with people seeking a rare midwestern historic experience or looking for a unique item in one of the many shops on Main Street. October is the most popular time to visit Galena, when the hills and valleys are covered with brilliant fall colors.

Experience nineteenth century life first hand by staying in one of the numerous historic district inns, bed and breakfast mansions, or the DeSoto House Hotel. All were built by men at the heights of their careers and wealth in the last century. Also a must, is a visit to the Galena/Jo Daviess County Historical Society & Museum on South Bench Street. The museum's multi-media slide show will give you an excellent look into the history of Galena and the people who shaped it.

Whatever time of year you visit Galena, slow down, relax and enjoy an historic experience.

Susan Pettey
Galena
March 1,1997

Whitefield View of Galena, Illinois 1856 (Opposite top) courtesy of the Galena/Jo Daviess County Historical Society & Museum Bottom: Modern view of the print.

2

GALENA, ILLINOIS

"Peace in Union," by Thomas Nast, 1895
courtesy of the Galena/Jo Daviess County Historical Society & Museum.

Captain Hezekiah H. Gear by John Mix Stanley, 1837,
courtesy of the Galena/Jo Daviess County Historical Society & Museum.

U.S. Grant Scout Pilgrimage Weekend: This year marked the 42nd annual gathering that celebrates Grant's birthday. The parade (oppsite left) is a tradition from the beginning.

October Country Fair Weekend. Arts & Crafts vendors gather in Grant Park for the biggest weekend in Galena.

8

Civil War encampment during
October Country Fair Weekend,
near U.S. Grant's home.

9

Civil War encampment October
Country Fair Weekend.

10

Grant Park Fountain.

PRIVATE RESIDENCES

Capt. Hezekiah H. Gear House. Gear made his fortune in the lead mines and donated large plots of land to the city for churches, cemeteries and schools. The house was built in 1855.

John Hellman House, an 1895 Queen Anne.

Nelson Stillman House, an 1858 Italianate.

Orrin Smith House, an 1852 Italianate.

William Ridd House, an 1891 Queen Anne.

Lucius S. Felt House, an 1851 home that was remodeled in the Second Empire style 1874.

Daniel F. Loveland House, an 1870 Italianate.

Vernacular architecture.

Vernacular architecture.

Guion Paul D'Zoya House, an 1838 Federal.

Cyrus Aldrich House, an 1846 Greek Revival.

James M. Strode House, an 1846 Greek Revival.

Hezekiah H. Gear House, an 1855 Italianate.

Bias Sampson House, an 1897 Queen Anne.

James Hudson House, an 1884 Queen Anne.

D. Harvey Lamberson House, an 1870 Vernacular

Galena's architectural details.

18

Reuben W. Brush House, c. 1837 Greek Revival.

OPEN AIR MARKET

Open Air Market, c. 1890 at the Old Market House.

Old Market House today.

**Old Market House, built 1845. An Illinois State Historic Site.
Continuous Open Air Markets were held from 1845-1910.**

23

Open Air Market today at the
Old Market House.

Aerial of the Old Market House.

CHURCHES

1850s view looking north through town.

27

Bench Street Churches.

There are several old cemeteries throughout town.

30

Left and above: Grace Episcopal Church, 1848.

A church's stain glass window.

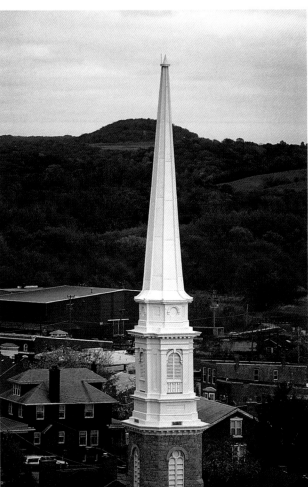

First Presbyterian Church, 1838.

First Methodist Church, 1857.

St. Matthew's Lutheran Church, 1864.

THEN AND NOW

General Grant's
Homecoming
August 18, 1865.

c.1852 view looking west with Route 20 in foreground.
Elihu B. Washburne House is in the lower right corner.

Elihu B. Washburne House, an 1844 Greek Revival.
An Illinois State Historic Site.

Sideview of Washburne House.

The Galena River, today and yesterday, 1852. During the river's heyday it was 250 ft. wide and numerous steamboats would dock at once.

Old Green Street Bridge
with the 1905 High School
in the background.

Main Street, yesterday and today.

Main Street, today and yesterday.

Alfred Mueller collection

43

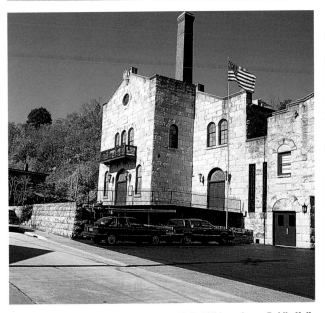

Turner Hall, 1874 used as a Public Hall.

Galena Public Library, 1907.

Feehan Hall, 1886. Today, it's the Art & Recreation Center.

East Galena Town Hall, 1872.

Galena Trolley Tour.

A surviving cobble stone street.

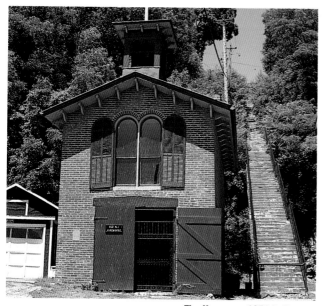

Fire House, an 1851 Italianate.

Main Street view.

45

Balzer and Casper Vogel, an 1867 Commercial Building.

A.J. Jackson House, an 1859 Italianate.
In 1865 it was given to U.S. Grant.

Main Street view.

Green Street Steps looking up from Main Street.

Old high school steps, 1920. *Richard Vincent collection*

High school steps, 1996.

47

Old Train Depot, an 1857 Italianate.

The Marine Hospital, an 1857 Italianate.

Old High School, 1905. It has been renovated into condominums.

U.S. Post Office, 1857. It was also a Custom House.

CHRISTMAS IN GALENA

Main Street shops.

Main Street Store detail.

The Old Train Depot, 1857. Today it houses the Chamber of
Commerce offices and Tourist Information Center.

Mistletoe Ball, held at Turner Hall in December.
A Galena/Jo Daviess County Historical Society & Museum fund-raiser.